EXPRESSIONS OF LIGHT

CHERIE BEIL

ILLUMIFY MEDIA GLOBAL
Littleton, Colorado

EXPRESSIONS OF LIGHT

Copyright © 2019 by Cherie Beil

All rights reserved. No part of this book may be reproduced in any form or by any means—whether electronic, digital, mechanical, or otherwise—without permission in writing from the publisher, except by a reviewer, who may quote brief passages in a review.

The views and opinions expressed in this book are those of the author and do not necessarily reflect the official policy or position of Illumify Media Global.

Published by
Illumify Media Global
www.IllumifyMedia.com
"Write. Publish. Market. *SELL!*"
Library of Congress Control Number: 978-1-947360-36-5

Paperback ISBN: 978-1-947360-30-3
eBook ISBN: 978-1-947360-31-0

Typeset by Art Innovations (http://artinnovations.in/)
Cover design by Debbie Lewis

Printed in the United States of America

Acknowledgment

In memory of my late husband, Frank Beil

1-23-1961 to 6-30-2011

We miss you.

For our daily struggles, pain, and earthly needs,

We rely on Jesus Christ.

"The lions may grow weak and hungry, but those who seek the Lord

Lack no good thing."

— Psalms 34: 10

Foreword

Rainbows are very complex and captivating.

They are glazed with brilliance, translucent in color and project a truth given to all.

They are a physical reminder made by a Spiritual Being of a promise made long ago.

It is a reassurance of hope and life.

It also reminds me of another promise made with an eternal resolve.

> "For God so loved the world, that he gave his only begotten Son,
> That whosoever believeth in him should not perish, but have everlasting life.
> For God sent not his Son into the world to condemn the world;
> But that the world through him might be saved."
>
> — John 3:16, 17 KJV

Spring Renewal

Fragrant aromas fill the air, in an awakening that marks the occasion of spring.

There is a sense of being rewarded with a second chance,

A time of revival for all.

    Fluorescent colors burst from blooms;

Holding secrets that they have been keeping all winter long.

The still cold air begins to heat and breathes new life into suspended hibernation.

    The sky is so big and far away,

As the grey is pushed out and replaced with a lucent blue.

    There is a quiet and peace all around

That does contrast the prevalent storms, which are now just a memory.

    And finally the time has arrived,

As tranquil joy emerges from the shedding confinement

To welcome a new season of spring renewal.

Signs of Faithfulness

God is faithful,

    Even when we are not.

The sun never fails to rise.

Water sprinkles the earth

    Continuously, as if set on a timer.

The seasons prevail unceasingly.

New stars are being formed

    As constant celestial lights to illuminate our imagination.

Life does abound everywhere

    Through blueprints placed in every seed.

The winds are a transporter of provisions,

    Created from nothing.

A delicate cocoon that envelops the earth,

To shield our existence, has not been duplicated.

The gardens of the deep are tended to with delicate hands

    That only the arms of God can reach.

Even in remote corners of the earth,

The smallest of creatures are equipped with provisions;

    Apart from Man's help.

Even through our own daily choices,

    Freedom to choose is a gift given

By a faithful God.

Using the Right Tools

What skills do our children really need to succeed us, and flourish?

Is it really what we say or do they measure our step?

Every opinion spoken or implied will be passed on,

Every nuance, bias or preference will be conveyed

    To the next generation.

Deed and word must match or they see right through us.

Our children need reality played out so desperately at home,

    If nowhere else.

By giving our children the tool of being accepted and approving of

    Their imperfect state, we can shave off years of struggles and

Difficulty that they need not encounter.

If we do not equip our children at home with the right tools,

How are they to know what to do when we are gone?

Remembering to be vulnerable,

    As honest as you can stand to be, and loving

Will equip them with a tool that will impact the future

    More than could ever be imagined.

Missing You

When you are gone, I count down the minutes,

    Hours and seconds until your return.

Life wants to push on, I want to stop

    And wait for you; but life will not let me.

All the hours we spend apart

    Add up to so many missed moments;

    Gone forever.

Exchanging details and long-distance recounts of the day

    Does not replace a shared brilliant sunset or a warm embrace.

It's not the big life-changing events that build our life together but

    Rather the simple, quiet moments.

It is moments like watching the silent stars fall from a dark sky;

    Seeing the rising harvest moon on an autumn evening;

Or awaiting a towering thunderstorm as it builds on the horizon,

    With anticipation of its thunderous arrival.

Time is slower and routing is void,

    As your absence reshapes my days.

Even though I am surrounded by others,

I fight the feeling of isolation and

Avoid the echoes of empty rooms.

I will always remain watchful for your return,

    Dread your next departure,

And anticipate the day when your furthest destination

Is our backyard.

I Am

I am a teacher of all I know; yet I am also the student.

I am a beacon of light, yet not a source of energy.

I encourage others with a hope that comes from an eternal light.

I care for the poor; yet I am in need daily.

I am weak but stronger than I know.

I am a resource in constant need of replenishment.

I am a dim reflection of a glory too radiant for an earthly destination.

I am patient only because of mercies I have received.

I am free; yet my freedom bore the highest cost.

I give love because I have known love.

I trust because I have been entrusted by One more faithful than I.

I can create, as I imitate the Originator of all creation.

I die daily, only to regain more vitality.

I have learned to respect through awe and wonders that are displayed throughout.

I know integrity, from the One who has walked my path.

I can see beyond today because of a vision of hope that was imparted.

I know who I am through the eyes of I AM.

Love

Love will reshape your paradigm
      As a sandscape image changes with every grain of colored sand
           That tumbles into place, perpetually able to renew.

Love does disrupt routine,
      Indifferent to schedules.

Love is designed to endure and deserving of allegiance;
      Constantly persuading you to give generously
      The gift of sacrifice.

Love is in constant motion,
      Taking us to unknown and foreign lands;
      Stretching us and coercing us to action.

Love does motivate greater,

Then the deepest sea of sorrow does suppress.

Love does reach beyond silence,

    Able to hold us to a mission of forgiveness;

        Reaffirming God's mercy, we receive new each day.

Love is able to withstand the greatest storms in life;

    Magnifying the good and vindicating the bad.

A life painted with the brush strokes of love is a fate we are all destined for;

    Worthy of the journey and detours it will take us.

Waves of Grief

When the tide comes in, it is an illusion of a gradual advancement.
The waters retreat, only to regain more and more ground
    With each converging wave;
        So it is with grief.
When jolted into a new reality, the waves of grief begin.
There is an alternating succession of overwhelming emotion.
The realization of a tremendous loss can be almost deafening.
Then just like a retreating wave, the agony does subside,
    Leaving you numb and cold;
Like being submerged in frigid tidal waters.
Battling a strong surge of sorrow can leave you feeling frail
    Like an empty shell that has been fractured and broken,
Tossed about by unmerciful waves.

When the next wave hits, it comes from nowhere,
    Unexpectedly, with such a powerful torrent
That even the bravest of us are left a weeping shambles.
When pain does ease and the rough seas relent,
    Emotions eventually are composed back into boundaries.
The alternating rising and falling sentiments
    Become more bearable.
For no one could withstand a tsunami of sorrow
    To overtake us all at once.
So it is with the waves of grief that protect us as we adapt,
    As we each must endure the rough seas of bereavement.

Patience and Perseverance

There is an anxiety that accompanies a long wait.

Illusive thoughts can hold you captive,

    And be misleading, while you endure.

Fortitude can be tedious, like hiking over rugged terrain.

Each uphill step feels more and more weighted

    As you scale your mountain.

When life's difficulties approach and strong gales of anxiety blow,

    You fight to keep your balance.

The intensity of the feeling of being so unsettled

    Will descend upon you like a wall of water,

Pouring down from heaven.

Life can be agonizing and almost unbearable
    As you remain watchful for a shelter of hope.
If you are unsure you can withstand life's storms,
    Remember they will eventually wear themselves out.
Like the sun emerging from dark skies,
    The light will engrave a sign of hope above.
Ominous fleeting clouds of adversity will be replaced
    With a prism of brilliant color and promise, seen by all.
For by persevering with patience,
    God is transforming us into His image
With every passing and invading storm.
    Until the storms do cease forever.

Distress

There are days when even the closest of friend
> Will turn on you.

There are moments you will feel abandoned
> By all.

There are times when betrayal
> Is prevalent.

When verbal blows feel as real
> As do physical ones.

When sadness hangs heavy,
> And tears come without warning.

Just as sudden large raindrops cast from heaven
> With their pounding unexpected arrival.

When you have been forsaken

    There is One who is faithful.

He is clothed in strength, armored in honor, creator of all.

    He is Love by nature, constant and unchanging, full of wisdom.

He is the light to the world, has no beginning nor ending.

He is not limited by earthly boundaries.

He cannot be measured by the universe, nor become void of mercies.

He will call the humble his friend.

So in your moments of distress, when the world has stranded you,

    Call on God.

For all who call out,

    There will be no distress cry left unanswered.

Hope

When darkness prevails and grey clouds begin to cry,

    Don't forget.

When the enemy comes to steal and pain is your only companion,

    Remember.

When loneliness echoes through a sterile room and time holds you hostage,

    Don't lose sight.

Remember the warmth of the sun

    And the ones you love.

Know the strength that is carried in the ones who love you.

So hope, have faith and endure.

Renew your mind, your soul and your inner strength

    By trusting in God.

Sleep knowing that your Angels are keeping watch.

For the hour will come when this too

    Will be another great race

That you are destined to win.

One Degree

The weight of one snowflake is immeasurable.

One raindrop will not create the smallest of puddles.

A single dark cloud in a sky filled with blue

    Hardly would be noticed.

A soft breeze cannot be calibrated.

It is hard to gauge a one-degree change in temperature.

However, a very trivial event that is magnified

    Of even the smallest entity can become calamity.

So also, with our lives, requiring moderation and equilibrium

    To maintain balance.

Measurable snow in feet can cascade into tragedy.

Droughts can frail the strongest of trees,

    Weakening them like aged and withered old men.

Spiraling winds moving at colossal speeds

    Can level the existence of all life in a given area,

Leaving only the remnants of a timeless scar.

We must hinge between the extremes to lengthen our stay.

Mindful to hasten through the biting cold,

    Scurry out of the sultry air, and try to live

In a peppery composite of moderation.

The Spoken Word

A single word spoken will set into motion

    Actions sometimes never intended.

A casual comment that can fall out of the mouth

    Does release power that extends far into the future.

The authority of life and even death

    Has been awarded to the spoken word.

Even the universe was created by the spoken word.

Sometimes a heart will reveal hope and truce to adversaries

    That soon will be revealed.

Other times a heart will expel a forbidding foe too powerful, it seems,

    To be conquered.

Then before the battle has even begun,
      It is already lost.
There is a truth in what we reveal from our heart
      Through the spoken word, which will reach into tomorrow.
We cannot recoil the words we have projected
      Once they have been sent out.
They will extend into our future and begin building bridges,
      Or tearing them down.
They can forecast a landscape of destruction ahead,
      Or restoration.
For it is vital that we recognize the power our words hold,
      Words that will entangle us into what lies ahead.

Lost Compass

It is hard to navigate,

    Having lost my compass.

Like finding my way through a blinding snowstorm

    Without a hand to hold.

It is like being far from home with no bearings in a vast, unfamiliar wilderness.

It is a struggle to stay grounded when strong winds have uprooted

    Our protective shelter.

For you were the compass that directed our ship;

    You were the life raft that God sent for us to cling to.

You were the shade tree that we rested underneath.

    You were the captain of our ship and the leader of our daily battles.

Your presence was a comfort, your smile was always welcome, your counsel respected,

    And your guidance essential.

You kept us moving when at times, uncertain of our destination.

    God has called you home and we feel lost without you.

My armor has been taken from me as I battle alone

    With no shield in front of me and my children behind me.

Losing you has left a cavern in my heart that the deepest ocean cannot fill.

    God does cry with me since you have been gone.

His tears have thundered down from the skies with heavy rains of sorrow and sadness.

He does comfort me in my consuming emptiness.

So now, be at peace and rest in the presence of the All Mighty.

For I will befriend an old foe, as patience and perseverance will walk with me,

    As I finish my race.

Until we walk together again.

Life's Story

Life does not end where we think it will;

    When it began.

Every journey is obscure and unique;

    No one can predict what turns a life's path may take.

Each path has its secrets that can only be revealed along the way.

No parent can envision for their newborn the storms or joys that lie ahead.

We each plan our passage in peaceful settings,

    Mapping our course for calm seas.

Then God takes our first draft of what we think life should be,

    And skillfully redefines each path.

No journey ends as originally charted.

As a mountain climber may have climbed the same mountain many times,

    No climb is ever the same.

We are so connected to other lives that we leave our fingerprint
    Everywhere we go.

Our lives continue, extending into other lives

As we impact others in ways that will not be revealed to us
    In this lifetime.

Like going down a river that seems to have no ending,
    With turns and bends seeming to go wherever it does choose.

Flowing with a continuous motion, never ceasing.

Our story of today will be retold for generations to come,

To influence future lives that now only exist in the mind of God.

So embrace the surprises in life and thank God for the failed plans.

For no one life story will be complete
    Until all the stories have been told.

Torch of Light

The truth is meant to awaken a darkened landscape,

    Like a full moon in a dark sky

That transforms blackness into awareness.

When truth is revealed, it will flare up like a sparkler on the Fourth of July,

    Leaving remnants everywhere it goes.

Expect the truth and await its arrival

    With the longing of a loved one's return from a long voyage.

Listen for truth as a whisper of honesty that does escalate

    Into a shout.

Share the truth as a dancing flame on a brightly lit candle,

    And it will ignite another to create more light.

Suppress the truth and an illness in the soul will break out,

    Spreading like a plague.

Deny the truth and an emptiness will grow,

    Which will cultivate a void too immense to ignore.

Extinguish the truth and you will stumble in darkness,

    Unable to have a vision for the future.

For the truth is not relevant for one.

    Rather the truth was established before the ages

For all, through the Son.

    So let the truth be in you.

Be a torch of light to spread to others, never to be extinguished,

    And always speak the truth.

Treasure and Fortune

We receive many gifts in life, but very few are remembered.

We have numerous joys, but rarely do they linger.

We are bestowed with countless responsibilites in a lifetime,

    But few that truly hold us accountable.

There are incalculable ways to spend a day, but there are very few ways

    A day can be spent that transforms the future.

Life is full of choices that require the sacrifice of our time;

    However, no time is sacrificed in vain when it is invested in another.

Our future is dependent upon the investment of ourselves

    Into the hearts and minds

Of those who would see us as their heros.

The greatest gift we can give to our children does not come from the world,

    But rather from within to protect them from the world.

There is not a more valuable gift in all the land that God can give

    Than the treasure and fortune that come wrapped up

In the gift of children.

Honor

Honor is earned when you keep your word.

Honor is acknowledged when you stand your ground.

Honor is awarded when you fight for principles.

Honor is given too often only after death has taken.

Honor is defended by protecting the defenseless.

Honor is a strength that is woven into the character of a few.

Honor is a respect granted only after a great sacrifice has been surrendered.

Honor is not a single event, rather a patchwork of events all sewn together,

    Creating a fiber of integrity that cannot be isolated.

Honor is often nearby, but obscure,

    Unable to be recognized until tragedy emerges.

Honor is blind to the council of the many, protecting the mission.

Honor is bringing to completion the required task,

    Indifferent of an approving committee.

Honor is a shield worn by only a handful

    Who do preserve life for the rest,

        Protecting the many who are unaware of the privileges possessed.

Honor is so often expected from many, displayed by the few

    Who choose to live and die clothed in an armor of honor.

Broken

There was once joy.

    There was once hope.

I can recount a purpose, not long ago.

    However, I have been broken into so many pieces that

I do not know if wholeness can ever be recreated back into totality.

    Or will there always remain jagged seams of brokenness?

My ship has been taken so far off course that I am in uncharted territories.

The rain is so heavy at times,

    I do not know where I am going.

Is there a plan for me?

    Or am I just a casualty of war?

Can restoration ever truly unveil and transform a sunken ship

    To its former beauty?

My memories of past joys are so faded,

    I cannot fully recount them.

It is so hard to see beyond the day

    When the horizon is so far away.

I must hang on to an unseen hope,

    And believe that this can be a new beginning,

Or my hope is in vain.

For I know that the sun does always rise,

    Even on the cloudiest of days.

What If?

What if we chose to turn the page in our minds

    And leave behind doubt and sorrow?

What if we chose to be jubilant

    And fight off depression?

What if we changed our thoughts

    Like we changed a channel?

What if we could choose peace and goodwill

    And let go of discontentment?

What would life be like if we could adjust our perceptions

    To alter our outcome?

What if, like an artist, we could choose what would go on the canvas?

    How different would the image be if we chose what to paint?

What if we chose to be faithful to our principles, regardless of our circumstances?

    Who would our children grow up to be?

What if we chose to look for God each day, to seek our plan

    As if it were our last?

What if we chose each moment to be a vessel of light

    And honor and truth?

Choose wisely, for every decision is another piece in our mosaic,

    Reflecting a pattern,

To seal our fate.

My Joyous Smile

I cannot help loving you.

You are so full of life that the world does not really awake

    Until you are awake.

The house is not fully at rest in the evening

    Until you are at rest.

Your eyes are as bright as a new snow

    On a clear winter morning.

Your innocence is as welcoming

    As a cool breeze on a hot summer afternoon.

The simplicity of life through your eyes does console me.

At times you are so elated with joy that you cannot contain it;

It is contagious.

You speak with such clarity and sincerity,

    Believing every word you say,

That you make me believe also.

You carry a peace with you and are willing to share

    With all in need.

There is such a gratitude you have,

    Just knowing that life is great, that it humbles me.

Your laughter does resonate in my heart

    With a healing quality.

My prayer for you is that as you grow,

    You never lose your exuberance for life,

And always remain my joyous smile.

Final Resting Place

When we become conscious of the closure of a life of someone we have known,

    There is a sudden restlessness and unease

For all the unspoken words and missed opportunities.

There is a terrible emptiness in the finality that surrounds death.

How do we perceive the vastness of the ocean waters or the multitude of stars in the sky?

And if we don't really know what it is that breathes new life into an unborn child,

    How can we truly grasp its worldly conclusion?

Maybe just knowing and valuing the existence of life,

    Is all God intended us to know.

Someday, when our souls have been reunited with our Maker,

    We will be radiant with awareness of what our lives have meant.

Then, what we once thought of as closure will be just the beginning

    Of an eternal, brilliant sunrise.

Signs of the Season

I know that time is just a deception, a measure in which we trick ourselves
    Into believing we have some control of its passing.
I also know that we measure sixty minutes by an hour passing,
    Twenty-four hours equivalent to one day and one night,
One sunrise and one sunset.
But shouldn't we measure each day by the number of breaths we take?
Or mark time by the consciousness of growth? The instant you suddenly become
    Aware that you have changed?
Not the number of seconds in a minute,
    But rather the number of hours, weeks or years between transformation?
Time should be measured by accomplishments achieved,
    Not by the signs of the seasons.
The timetable we live by should be a perpetual rhythm of self-awareness.
The celebration of each attained goal,
And the opportunity each breath of life offers.

Faith

Faith does not come when all is well.

Faith begins to take shape and grow,

    When calamity strikes.

Faith is finding out what is really trustworthy.

Faith is having a peace,

    When the world around you is at war.

Faith is forging ahead,

    Even when you are lost.

Faith is tested,

    When you have nothing else to rely on.

Faith is knowing in time of need,

      You will be granted mercy.

Faith is believing for clarity,

      When you can only see the sun,

            Through a dull smoky haze,

                  From a fire close at hand.

Faith is an expectation,

      Knowing that there is a divine plan,

And a peace that you are securely held in the hands of The Most High.

Peace in Uncertain Times

Peace is a rare commodity in these uncertain days.

Darkness is beginning to engulf the world as the lines

    Between right and wrong are blurred.

Compromise with things that used to be unthinkable

    Is now a coveted skill.

Lies, whispered in secret

    Are now broadcast as truth in the noonday sun.

The mask of deceit worn by so many comes with a price.

The eternal debt is not considered by those

    Who have their eye on the temporal prize.

True peace cannot be negotiated or bought,

    But is a gift that can only be given by the Prince of Peace.

What About You?

Where is integrity?
> Honor is void.

Our leaders are like weakened trees with no roots to sustain them through

Torrential winds of truth.

They do not escape.

Older generations have become tolerant of decay in our families
> That has shipwrecked and abandoned our children.

Our children are searching and malnourished
> For principles, values and guidance that we do not provide.

Where is honesty?

What cost are we willing to pay for telling the truth?
> Or does the spin fix our problems, like the instant society we have created?

Who earnestly strives for a degree in righteousness?
> Do we indebt ourselves for more knowledge or more wisdom?

Are we leaders,

    Or do we now follow?

Does the pushing of the crowds make us go through the doors of compromise,

    Or do we turn and resist?

Who will stand against evil,

    Or does this come with too high a price tag?

Who will remember to end

    Better than when they began?

To strive for an outcome that does not center on self-gain, but rather glory for a

    Higher cause

That will outlast the universe.

God is calling throughout the land

    To see who will respond to his challenge for righteousness.

Echoes are His reply.

What about you?

www.ingramcontent.com/pod-product-compliance
Lightning Source LLC
Chambersburg PA
CBHW051359110526
44592CB00023B/2887